Semitrucks

Martha E.H. Rustad
AR B.L.: 3.0
Points: 0.5   MG

HORSEPOWER

SEMITRUCKS

by Martha E. H. Rustad

Reading Consultant:

Barbara J. Fox

Reading Specialist

North Carolina State University

Capstone
press

Mankato, Minnesota

Blazers is published by Capstone Press,
151 Good Counsel Drive, P.O. Box 669, Mankato, Minnesota 56002.
www.capstonepress.com

Library of Congress Cataloging-in-Publication Data
Rustad, Martha E. H. (Martha Elizabeth Hillman), 1975–
    Semitrucks / by Martha E. H. Rustad.
    p. cm.—(Blazers. Horsepower)
    Summary: "Describes semitrucks, their main features, and how they
are used"—Provided by publisher.
    Includes bibliographical references and index.
    ISBN-13: 978-1-4296-0827-5 (hardcover)
    ISBN-10: 1-4296-0827-7 (hardcover)
    1. Tractor trailer combinations—Juvenile literature. I. Title. II. Series.
TL230.15.R87 2008
629.224—dc22   2007005407

Editorial Credits
Christopher L. Harbo, editor; Jason Knudson, set designer; Patrick D.
    Dentinger, book designer; Jo Miller, photo researcher

Photo Credits
Capstone Press/Karon Dubke, cover, 10–11, 14–15
Corbis/Momatiuk–Eastcott, 28–29; Richard T. Nowitz, 22–23;
    TH-Foto/zefa, 24–25
Dreamstime/Fernando Rodrigues, 8–9; Linda & Colin Mckie, 21
Folio, Inc./David Frazier, 6
Peter Arnold/Ron Gilling, 20
Photri-MicroStock, 27; J. Powell, 10; M. Gibson, 13
Shutterstock/Joy Brown, 26; Karl R. Martin, 16–17; Kevin Norris, 12;
    Kim Seidl, 7; Robert Pernell, 18–19
SuperStock, Inc./Tom Rosenthal, 4–5

**Capstone Press thanks Darcy Marie, Vice President, Transportation
Center for Excellence, Eagan, Minnesota, for her assistance in
preparing this book.**

1 2 3 4 5 6 12 11 10 09 08 07

TABLE OF CONTENTS

THE LONG HAUL

A fully loaded semitruck rumbles down a highway. Blowing snow covers the road. The truck driver uses all of her skills to deliver her load on time.

Thousands of semitrucks crisscross
the country every day. They deliver
everything from apples to video games.

BLAZER FACT

Drivers keep their trucks within inches of other trucks as they back up to loading docks.

Loading dock

48-6609

7

SEMITRUCK DESIGN

The tractor is the front part of a semitruck. The driver steers the semitruck from the cab. Some tractors have sleeper cabs with beds, kitchens, and TVs inside.

Cab

Sleeper cab

Tractors have wide tires attached to the front and rear axles. Front axles have two big tires. Rear axles have two or four tires. Tractors hauling the heaviest loads have two rear axles.

Rear axles

Fifth wheel

Tractors pull semitrailers with
their fifth wheel. The fifth wheel is
at the back of the tractor. A kingpin
on the front of the trailer locks into
the fifth wheel.

BLAZER FACT

Semitrucks pulling two semitrailers are called doubles. Triples pull three semitrailers.

Huge diesel engines power semitrucks. Some engines have as much as 600 horsepower. These powerful engines pull loads weighing up to 80,000 pounds (36,000 kilograms).

BLAZER FACT

A semitruck's fuel tanks hold up to 300 gallons (1,136 liters) of diesel fuel.

SEMITRUCK PARTS

Semitrailer

Sleeper cab

Spare tire

Rear axles

Fuel tank

Exhaust pipes

Rearview mirrors

Tractor

Wide front tire

BIG LOADS

Semitrucks carry almost any kind of cargo. Tankers hold liquids such as milk or gasoline. Tankers can be heated or cooled to keep liquids a certain temperature.

Semitrucks also carry containers
and pull flatbeds. Containers are large
boxes. They often hold goods shipped
from other countries. Flatbeds carry
loads like heavy vehicles or lumber.

Semitrucks move loads most other vehicles could never pull. Some semitrucks even move whole houses.

ROLLING DOWN THE HIGHWAY

Semitrucks travel long distances. Drivers stop at truck stops along the way. These large fuel stations let drivers park their trucks, eat a meal, and rest.

Semitrucks roll down highways
24 hours a day, seven days a week.
Semitrucks make sure people have
the goods they need every day.

BLAZER FACT

Laws state that truck drivers can drive up to 11 hours in a row. Then they must rest for 10 hours.

18 WHEELIN' DOWN THE OPEN ROAD!

GLOSSARY

axle (AK-suhl)—a rod in the center of a wheel; axles turn wheels.

cargo (KAR-goh)—objects carried by a ship, aircraft, or other vehicle

container (kuhn-TAYN-ur)—a box that can be loaded onto a semitruck; containers can hold many types of goods.

diesel (DEE-zuhl)—a heavy fuel that burns to make power; many semitrucks run on diesel fuel.

flatbed (FLAT-bed)—a long, flat trailer used to carry cargo

kingpin (KING-pin)—a metal rod used to join a trailer to a tractor

tanker (TANG-kur)—a vehicle designed to carry large amounts of liquid

READ MORE

Molzahn, Arlene Bourgeois. *Trucks and Big Rigs.* Transportation and Communication Series. Berkeley Heights, N.J.: Enslow, 2003.

Ransom, Candice. *Big Rigs.* Pull Ahead Books. Minneapolis: Lerner, 2005.

Stille, Darlene R. *Big Rigs.* Transportation. Minneapolis: Compass Point Books, 2002.

INTERNET SITES

FactHound offers a safe, fun way to find Internet sites related to this book. All of the sites on FactHound have been researched by our staff.

Here's how:

1. Visit *www.facthound.com*
2. Choose your grade level.
3. Type in this special code **1429608277** for age-appropriate sites. You may also browse by clicking on letters, or by clicking on pictures and words.
4. Click on the **Fetch It** button.

FactHound will fetch the best sites for you!

INDEX